Paper into Pots

Paper into Pots
and other fun objects
using hand-made recycled paper
and papier-mâché techniques

GERRY COPP

SEARCH PRESS

First published in Great Britain 1994

Search Press Limited
Wellwood, North Farm Road,
Tunbridge Wells, Kent TN2 3DR

Copyright © Search Press Ltd. 1994

Reprinted 1995

Photographs by Search Press Studios, with the exception of that on page 41, which is by James Copp.

To James Copp, without whom none of this would have been possible.

ISBN 0 85532 772 3

745.54 COP

Printed in Spain by Elkar S. Coop, 48012, Bilbao.

Contents

INTRODUCTION

There is so much paper in modern society that we hardly notice it! It has hundreds of uses, from books and newspapers to packaging, computer print-outs, greetings cards, and gift wrap, and because of mass production the quantities of waste paper produced are enormous.

Today, as concern rises over the waste of raw materials, the idea of recycling paper has become widely accepted. This process need not be limited to factories, because by making use of basic techniques which have been used to make paper for centuries, it can be carried out very successfully in the average kitchen.

Paper is made when the fibres of a plant are separated, suspended in water, and then recombined into a flat, even sheet. The Chinese discovered this process in the second century AD, before which paper had been made by flattening plants, such as papyrus, to form sheets. The secret of true paper-making was jealously guarded, but as a result of espionage this secret got out, and the art of paper-making began to spread.

Before the paper-making process was mechanised in the late eighteenth century it was a slow and labour-intensive process. Paper was valuable and people were eager to reuse it: this led to the development of the craft of papier mâché.

Imported papier-mâché goods such as boxes, toys and plates arrived in Europe from the Far East. The French were the first European nation to produce commercial papier mâché, which reached the height of its popularity in Europe at around 1770. During a period of about a hundred years there were papier-mâché factories across Europe as well as in Russia, England, and, later, in America.

The variety of items was staggering and ranged from the mundane to the fantastic. Small items such as snuff boxes, pencil cases and dolls' heads were made, as well as larger objects like lamp stands, tea trays and a range of architectural mouldings. Some manufacturers even went so far as to make furniture from papier mâché, while others went to the opposite extreme and produced unlikely items such as a watch and all its internal workings. Perhaps the most remarkable of all was an entire church, which was built in Norway.

However, when increased mechanisation in paper-making led to an abundant supply of paper products, papier mâché began to be replaced by other, less time-consuming things. As a result the crafts of paper-making and papier mâché began to decline.

In recent years interest in both crafts has been rekindled and they are once again beginning to flourish. There are various reasons why many artists and craftspeople have chosen to work with these techniques: both of them are cheap to do and the equipment and materials needed can usually be found around the home. Also, both methods are versatile and easy to learn.

My own introduction to paper-making, and to basic papier mâché, came when I was a child. However, it was concern for the environment that led me back to both crafts as an adult. I began to experiment, and soon found that I could make highly decorative objects by collaging sheets of hand-made, recycled paper on to papier-mâché forms. Also, unlike with traditional methods, I found that this technique had the added advantage of requiring no paints or dyes to provide a decorative finish.

I continued to experiment with different types of finish by using other materials as well, such as sweet-wrappers and coloured foils. I also began to experiment with irregular surfaces, and to make more complicated forms.

This book explains the basic techniques and also shows how they can be combined. I hope that this will not only inspire you to try some of the ideas yourself, but will also encourage you to make your own objects from recycled paper.

The process may seem to take a lot of time, but you will find that it really is great fun to create beautiful objects out of what might once have been described as 'a load of rubbish'!

MAKING PAPER FOR COLLAGE

The paper-making process described in this chapter has been developed as a means of converting coloured waste paper into sheets of hand-made, recycled paper suitable as basic materials for collage. The sheets may not be of as high a quality as those made by more complex processes, such as those used to produce hand-made writing paper, but the technique is nevertheless simple, fast, and effective.
I prefer to use papers I have made myself by recycling for collage, not only for environmental reasons, but also because they are better suited to tearing and pasting, particularly where the subject has a curved surface.

Tearing machine-made papers into small, complicated shapes is difficult, not only because the sheets tend to be too thick but also because the mechanised process pulls the fibres in one direction only, which gives the paper a definite grain. Tearing across this grain is difficult and, more often than not, results in a shape with unwanted jagged edges.

Similarly, a machine-made paper pasted on to anything other than a flat surface creates an unattractive, bumpy finish. By using hand-made, recycled papers these problems can be overcome, and the time spent making the sheets is more than rewarded by the resulting supply of unique, coloured materials at little or no cost.

Materials and equipment

If you use coloured waste paper as your raw material there is no need for paints or dyes. Dyeing paper is a messy and complicated process which means buying dyes or paints which may well be expensive. However, with a bit of imagination and persistence it is possible to obtain coloured waste paper quite easily. Ask places such as libraries, art centres and theatres to save out-of-date coloured leaflets and posters for you. Printers are usually happy, if a little puzzled by the request, to save coloured offcuts left over from the trimming and finishing of leaflets, posters, and other print jobs.

Be wary of papers with plastic coatings, or those used in glossy magazines and brochures. These are unsuitable for recycling because they are difficult to break down. They may also contain unpleasant chemicals.

On the other hand, the black print on coloured leaflets is sometimes only partially broken down during the recycling process, and may remain in the new sheet of paper as an attractive speckle. Sometimes whole letters, or even words, may survive the recycling process and be visible in the finished sheets. Whether this is deliberate, or merely the result of a 'happy accident', it often adds a unique charm to the work.

If you really cannot find the necessary range or quantities of coloured paper it is, of course, possible to recycle machine-made papers. However, buying paper in this way not only defeats the object of making something from waste products, but can also work out expensive. You will find that spending a little time hunting for reliable sources of waste paper will be well worth the effort.

Some types of paper may fade after a relatively short period of time, but you can avoid this problem by using relatively good-quality raw materials. For instance, I always avoid sugar paper because it fades very quickly.

You can estimate how permanent a particular colour is likely to be by seeing how much dye comes out of the paper when you tear it and soak it in water at the beginning of the recycling process. If the water looks very discoloured, it will probably be better, in the long run, to use something else.

Materials and equipment.

You will need

A mould
Coloured waste paper
Plastic containers
A food liquidiser
A jug
Reusable kitchen cloths, or nappy liners
An oblong washing-up bowl, or similar
Two sheets of hardboard
A pile of old newspapers
An iron

You will find most of the equipment you will need for paper-making around the home. Each item in the list above is described and explained in the text that follows.

The only specialist piece of equipment is a mould. This is a flat, sieve-like object which is used to reconstruct the separated fibres of the paper pulp into flat sheets.

Paper is traditionally made with a mould and a deckle. A mould is a rectangular frame with a mesh stretched over it. A deckle is a frame which is the same size as the mould, but without the mesh. The two are used together, with the deckle on top of the mould. The resulting sheets of paper have straight, regular edges.

I prefer to use a mould without a deckle, though, which means that my sheets of paper have uneven edges; I like the look of these. This sort of finish might not be appropriate for writing paper, but it is not a problem for sheets which I am going to tear up and use as collage to decorate objects.

You can buy moulds and deckles in art and craft shops, but you can also make them easily and cheaply at home. I make my own from artists' stretchers which I buy from a local art shop.

As the name suggests, stretchers are rectangular frames used by artists to stretch canvas as a surface for oil painting. They are purpose-made in four parts, each of which having mitred corners, that are easily slotted together to form rectangular frames of various sizes. No nails or glues are needed to join the pieces of the stretcher, which, even when made from untreated wood, will last for years.

If you prefer to make your own mould you will need to use four pieces of wood joined together in a rectangle with waterproof glue, or rust-proof nails, or both. The frame must be small enough to fit into an oblong washing-up bowl or similar container.

To complete the mould, attach a fine mesh to the frame. I have found that the most successful

Make your own simple mould from a wooden stretcher – the one below is ready to be slotted together. Then simply attach the mesh with drawing pins.

material is the aluminium mesh which is sold in most DIY stores for car-body repairs. It is easily available, and comes in sheets measuring 25 x 20.5cm (10 x 8in). You may need to trim it to size, but it is easy to attach to the wooden frame with flat-headed drawing pins.

As a rough guide to the quantities of waste paper required, ten A5 (8 x 6in) pages will make about the same number of sheets of hand-made paper.

Techniques

The first step is to tear the paper into pieces about 4.5cm (2in) square and soak them in water for a few hours. Any convenient container is suitable for this part of the process; I find old ice-cream tubs or large margarine containers are ideal.

When the paper has become soggy, put a little into the liquidiser and then top it up with water from the jug. Liquidise the mixture until it forms a smooth pulp.

Take great care when using large quantities of water with a liquidiser. There is always the danger of electric shock, and I prefer to use a circuit-breaker at all times. There is also a potential danger to hands and fingers from the spinning blades of the liquidiser, and children should always be supervised.

It is easy to clean a liquidiser after a paper-making session and return it to its normal use in the kitchen. However, if you are planning to do a lot of paper-making, it is probably worth having a liquidiser just for that purpose.

If you do not want to use a liquidiser it is possible to make paper without one. To do this, first tear the paper into pieces, soak them in water for at least twenty-four hours, then pound them with a large pestle and mortar (or a stout piece of wood in a bucket) until reduced to a pulp. However, I have found that paper which has been made in this way is never really smooth, and tends to be rather disappointing, especially as a material for collage.

When you have produced your pulp you will

need an oblong washing-up bowl or other large plastic container to hold the mixture of pulped paper and water. The bowl must be larger than the frame, and should be at least 15cm (6in) deep.

The reusable carriers (kitchen cloths or nappy liners) are used to receive each sheet of wet paper as it comes off the mould. This way you gradually build up a stack of alternating carriers and papers as each sheet is produced. The process is called couching. Smooth kitchen cloths, cut into pieces slightly larger than the frame, are ideal. Nappy liners work just as well as carriers, are cheaper, and last longer, but either of these can be washed out and used several times.

By placing wooden boards above and below the completed stack of papers and carriers, you can apply pressure and squeeze out excess water without damaging the sheets of paper. The boards need to be at least as big as the carriers, and should be fairly rigid. Plywood and hardboard are both ideal. You could use a heavy book or a printing press, but I prefer to stand on the stack and squeeze the excess water out with my own weight!

After pressing out the water, peel the papers and the cloth carriers apart and leave each sheet to dry, still on its carrier. It is useful to lay the papers and the carriers on sheets of old newspaper during this part of the process, which will take up to twelve hours if the drying is at room temperature. You can speed the process up if you like by ironing the papers. (Only papers made on kitchen cloths can be dried in this way, though, because nappy liners will melt!) Cover the damp paper with a cloth and iron it until it is dry enough to be peeled away from the carrier. You can then iron the sheet of paper until it is dry.

The surface of paper which has been ironed in this way will be smooth and shiny when dry.

A stunning range of sheets of hand-made paper made from coloured waste.

Making hand-made paper – step by step

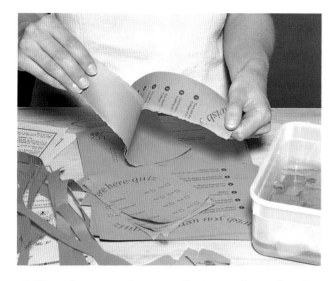

1 Tear the paper into small pieces about the size of a postage stamp. Soak in water for a few hours, or until soft.

2 Put a small handful of the paper into the liquidiser. Top up with water to the maximum indicated. Put on the lid, and liquidise for about ten seconds. If there is too much paper in the liquidiser, the motor will labour, in which case you should remove some paper before continuing. Do not run the liquidiser for more than thirty seconds without allowing it to rest, or the motor may overheat.

3 When the paper has been reduced to a smooth pulp, pour it into a washing-up bowl which is about two-thirds full of tepid water.

4 Place one pressing board on top of a newspaper and place six damp cloth carriers on top of the board. The cloths must be flat, and directly on top of each other. These cloths will act as padding, and will make it easier to get the sheet of wet paper off the mould.

Making hand-made paper – step by step

5 Stir the pulp in the bowl so that the little particles are evenly suspended in the water. Lower the mould, with the drawing-pin heads facing upwards, to the bottom of the bowl.

6 Lift the mould quickly out of the bowl in a horizontal position. A layer of fibres will be trapped on the mesh. When most of the water seems to have drained away, tilt the frame to allow the rest to run off.

7 Hold the mould above the pile of carriers and turn it over so that the layer of pulp comes into contact with the top cloth.

8 Carefully but firmly press the back of the mesh to transfer the wet pulp on to the pile of cloth carriers.

9 Lift the mould smoothly away from the cloths, leaving the layer of pulp behind. The most common reasons for failure at this stage are that the mesh was not pressed hard enough in the previous stage, or that the pulp was allowed to drain on the mesh for too long.

10 Cover the newly formed sheet of wet paper with a damp cloth carrier. Make sure that it is completely flat, as any creases will affect the surface of the next sheet of paper. Now repeat stages 5–10. You can make about five sheets of paper from one lot of pulp. The amount of pulp in the bowl is obviously reduced each time you make a sheet of paper, so add some fresh pulp when the layer on the mould gets so thin that the mesh can clearly be seen through it. Add it gradually to avoid making sheets that are too thick, and stir the mixture each time.

11 When you have made as many sheets of paper as you need, cover the last sheet with a damp cloth carrier.

12 Place the second pressing board on top of the stack.

Making hand-made paper – step by step

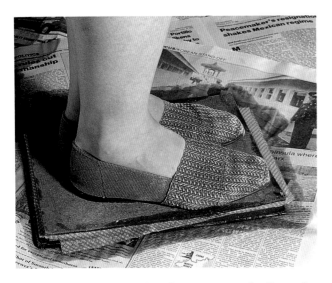

13 Take the stack of papers, including the boards, outside. Now stand on top of the stack to squeeze out as much water as possible! (Do not jump or stamp on the stack, as this may damage the paper.) If you live in a flat and have to do this indoors, put a thick layer of newspaper down first!

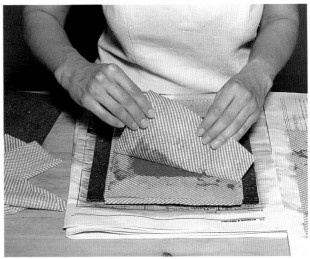

14 Take the stack back indoors and remove the top board. Carefully peel off each cloth carrier, with a sheet of paper attached, and lay it on to a sheet of newspaper to dry. The wet paper may stick to the cloth on top of it as well as to the one below. If it does, carefully ease it back on to the bottom cloth.

15 The paper will take about twelve hours to dry at room temperature. When dry, you will find that it peels from the cloth quite easily.

16 I always iron my dry sheets of paper as I find them easier to handle for collage. You can put the iron directly on to the paper, but it is a good idea to protect the ironing surface.

When I have finished using a particular colour of pulp I strain, dry and store it, or throw it away. Never pour pulp down the sink, as it will cause a blockage.

Decorative sheets

By developing the basic techniques of paper-making you can create a wide range of decorative papers. On these pages you can see just a few of the many possibilities – I am sure you can think of others.

One of the things I enjoy about making recycled paper is experimenting, because I know I can try out new ideas without worrying about wasting expensive materials.

Multi-coloured paper

Multi-coloured or speckled sheets can be made by mixing different coloured pulps. If both pulps are very fine they will combine to produce a third colour. For example, if you mix a fine yellow pulp with a fine blue pulp, you will get a sheet of green paper. However, it is quite difficult to predict how things will turn out because one colour will often dominate the other. The paper also tends to change colour as it dries, so the rich purple you think you have made may end up as a dusty maroon when it is dry!

Varying the time for which different colours are liquidised produces a range of pulps made up of smaller or larger fragments. By mixing these together in varying proportions you can make an endless variety of attractive speckled sheets.

Laminating

Another effective technique is to laminate or layer two different coloured sheets. To do this, make the first sheet as described in the step-by-step instructions, but instead of covering the newly formed sheet of paper with a cloth, make a second

Multi-coloured and laminated sheets of paper.

Paper containing tea-leaves (left) and threads (right).

Sheets of paper laminated with leaves (left) and string (right).

sheet of paper from a different-coloured pulp and place it on top of the first. The two sheets of paper will dry as one.

By drawing with a finger on the second sheet of paper while it is still on the mould, you can remove areas of pulp. When this second sheet is placed on top of the first, parts of the first sheet will show through where the pulp has been removed. You could add several more layers to build up a complex pattern, or a picture.

By varying the laminating technique, flat objects such as leaves, feathers and string can be sandwiched between pairs of sheets. Lay the object on the first sheet of paper and place the second sheet on top. This traps the object between the sheets, and a raised impression of the object will appear on the top sheet. I find that this technique is most effective when using fine white pulp and an object with bold outlines.

Adding fibres, threads, leaves, etc.

Interesting papers can be made by adding small particles to the mixture of water and pulp. Tea leaves, chopped herbs, and short threads are all ideal. The mesh traps the paper fibres and will also trap whatever has been added. This technique will only work if small particles are used, as larger or heavier things will fall off the paper as it dries.

You could combine these techniques to produce more complicated designs. For instance, you could make a first sheet of scented herb paper and place a leaf on top of it. A second sheet could be laid on top of this and sections removed to reveal parts of the leaf below. The possibilities really are endless, and an afternoon spent experimenting is bound to result in your producing some exciting and decorative sheets of hand-made paper. You can then collage these on to your papier-mâché objects to add texture and interest.

MAKING A PAPIER-MÂCHÉ BASE

I make papier-mâché objects which I decorate with collages of hand-made coloured papers. Newspaper is a traditional source of material for the papier-mâché part of the process, but I prefer not to use it because the printing inks contain acid which may attack the decorative surface. I prefer to use other sorts of waste paper such as old envelopes, writing paper, paper offcuts, and computer printouts.

Layering and *pulping* are the two techniques used in papier mâché.

The layering technique is familiar to most people through childhood memories of layering sticky paper on to a balloon, while the pulp method involves reducing waste paper to a pulp in a liquidiser and combining the pulp with paste.

The techniques produce very different end results. Layering produces a smooth, thin surface, like porcelain in appearance, whereas pulped objects are thicker, rougher, and more akin to pottery. Although the pulp process may seem more complicated, and does require more equipment, I find that it is much quicker than layering. I use pulp for making unsupported shapes such as bowls and plates, where strength is of paramount importance.

When I want a smooth surface – for instance, when making a clock, or mirror frame – I use the layering method.

Materials and equipment

Most of the equipment needed for papier mâché can be found around the home.

Layering method

Waste paper
Container for paste
Cling film
Indelible pen
Plastic spatula
Old spoon
Wallpaper paste

Pulp method

In addition to the above you will need

A liquidiser
Colander
Old cloth – about 50 x 50cm (18 x 18in)
A washing-up bowl

Paste

Everyone who uses papier mâché seems to have a different recipe for paste! Many people use flour and water, while some add linseed oil and oil of cloves. I have found cellulose wallpaper paste ideal. For the layering method I mix the paste until it has a milky consistency. For the pulp method, however, I mix the paste to the maximum strength stated by the manufacturer.

Fungicide warning

Do take care when using wallpaper paste containing a fungicide. Always follow the manufacturers' safety advice, and if you have sensitive skin, remember to wear gloves.

Moulds for papier mâché

When choosing an existing object as a mould it is important to consider how you are going to get the dry papier-mâché form off afterwards! Under-cut shapes are best avoided because the only way to get the papier mâché off them is to cut it with a knife. The pieces then have to be glued together, which can be rather difficult to do well. (I have to use this technique on my big globe-shaped pots.) Open forms, like bowls and plates, are much easier to use.

A mould can be made from any material, but the papier mâché will take several days to dry, so do not use objects that you may need in the meantime! I have collected old bowls, jars, vases, and even plastic lampshades for use as moulds.

When using an existing object as a mould, you will need to put a barrier between the mould and the papier mâché to stop them sticking together. I use cling film, which I find is easier to apply and more reliable than the petroleum jelly which is often recommended. You can draw a line on the cling film with an indelible pen or marker to show where the rim of the bowl will be. This line will be transferred to the papier-mâché form as it dries, making it easy to trim the bowl to an even finish if need be.

If you want to create your own simple shapes for use as moulds, such as the fish on page 48, you can easily make them from plaster of Paris. Mould-making is not difficult, and will extend the range of forms that you can use. It is also possible to make cardboard formers, instead of moulds, on to which papier mâché and hand-made papers can be laid to make boxes, frames, clocks, and even sculptures.

Putting the papier mâché in an airing cupboard or some other warm place can reduce the drying time from a week or more to just a few days.

The versatility of papier mâché is astounding. Here I describe the basic techniques and suggest some developments, but I hope you will experiment and find new ways of using the medium.

A selection of moulds: vase, bowl, bottle, jar, old lampshade...

Layering method – step by step

1 Tear the waste paper into small pieces approximately 5cm (2in) square.

2 Stretch the cling film tightly over the inverted mould, taking care not to leave any gaps.

3 Use a piece of paper to measure from the top of the mould (*i.e.* the bottom of the bowl) down to where the edge of the bowl is to be, and draw a line on the cling film with the indelible marker. (If I want a rough edge I miss this stage out).

4 Dilute the paste to a milky consistency and dip the pieces of paper into it, making sure that you smear both sides. It is best not to add large quantities of paper to the paste as the paper will tend to stick together and the pieces will become hard to separate.

 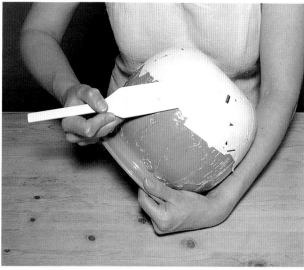

5 Start the first layer at the top of the mould. Gradually cover the cling film with overlapping pieces of paper until you have covered the marked line. Repeat the process, working in different directions, until there are three or four layers. Make sure that each layer is smooth, and that any air bubbles are pressed out.

6 Allow the papier mâché to dry thoroughly before repeating stages 4 and 5 and building up additional layers. When the layers are dry, ease the papier mâché from the mould. I find it helps to break the vacuum by inserting a plastic spatula between the mould and the papier mâché.

An undecorated layered bowl with its mould.

Pulp method – step by step

1 Tear the waste paper into small pieces about the size of a postage stamp, and soak it in water for a few hours.

2 Put a little soaked paper into the liquidiser and fill it with water to the 'maximum' line. Blend for about ten seconds. Pulp for papier mâché need not be as fine as for paper-making.

3 Stand the colander in a tray or bowl, then place the cloth in the colander and pour the pulp into it.

4 Gather the ends of the cloth together and squeeze it gently. When the water has been squeezed out of the pulp, what remains should be moist but not runny.

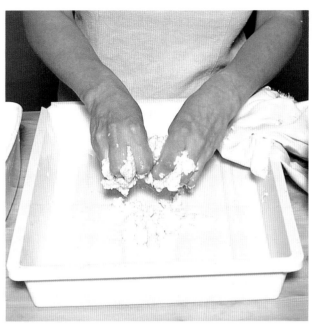

5 Tip the moist pulp into a bowl and rub it, as if rubbing fat into flour, to break it up into small pieces.

6 Add the paste, which should be thick but not sticky. Squeeze the paste through the pulp until it is evenly distributed.

7 Stretch the cling film tightly over the mould, and do not leave any gaps. (As I often use this mould, I have marked permanent guidelines on it at two different levels.)

8 Measure from the top of the mould to where the edge of the bowl is to be, and draw a line on the cling film. If you want a rough edge, miss this stage out.

Pulp method – step by step

9 Starting at the top of the mould, apply small quantities of pulp to it: about 0.75cm (⅓in) thick. Smooth the pulp carefully, just covering the line, then leave it to dry. If it is too runny it will slide off; if too dry it will be difficult to smooth flat. Adjust the quantities of paste and pulp to get the right consistency.

10 When the papier mâché is dry, prise it gently away from the mould. It helps to break the vacuum by inserting a plastic spatula between the mould and the papier mâché.

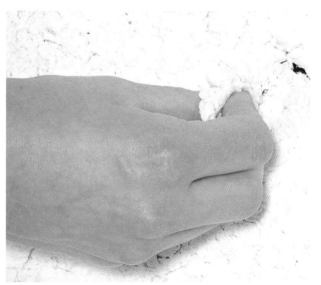

11 A faint image of the marker line will have transferred itself to the inside of the bowl. Now, using this line as a guide, trim the edge of the bowl.

12 Finally, fill any large cracks with a mixture of pulp and paste, and leave the bowl to dry for about a day before going on to the decorating stage.

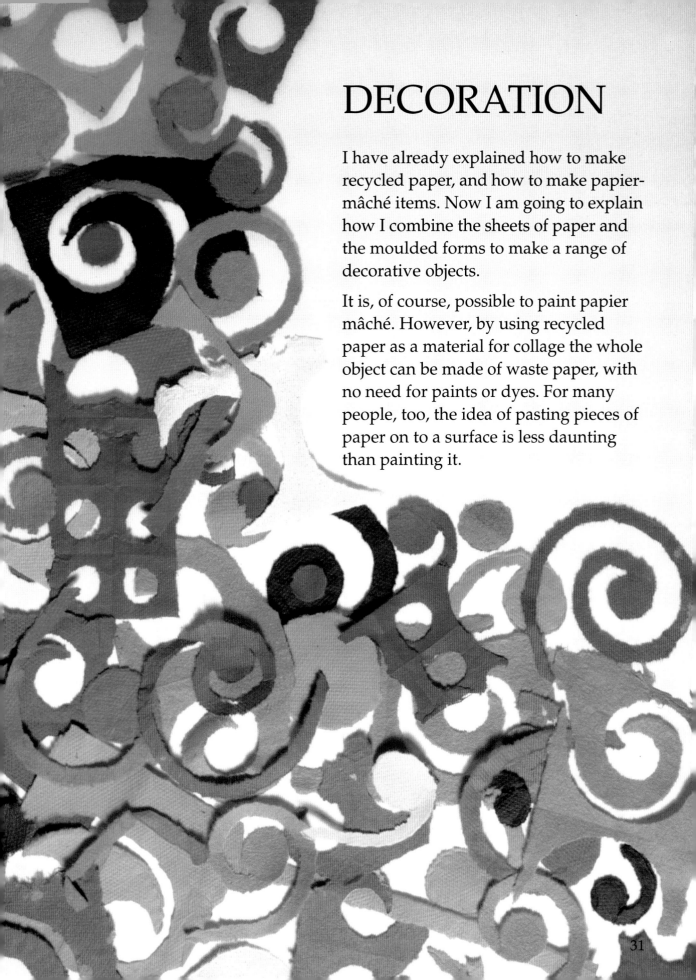

DECORATION

I have already explained how to make recycled paper, and how to make papier-mâché items. Now I am going to explain how I combine the sheets of paper and the moulded forms to make a range of decorative objects.

It is, of course, possible to paint papier mâché. However, by using recycled paper as a material for collage the whole object can be made of waste paper, with no need for paints or dyes. For many people, too, the idea of pasting pieces of paper on to a surface is less daunting than painting it.

Surface pattern

My technique involves tearing shapes from sheets of paper and pasting them on to a form made of papier-mâché, cardboard, or sometimes wood. By folding the sheets of paper several times you can save time and tear out multiples of a given shape.

You will need

Scissors
PVA glue
Medium-sized paintbrush
Sheets of hand-made papers
Papier-mâché, wooden, or cardboard form

Although tearing out a specific shape might seem difficult at first, it will soon become quite easy. (I find it much easier to tear a circle from a piece of paper than to draw it!) Initially it may help to draw complicated shapes on to the paper before trying to tear them, but after a bit of practice this will no longer be necessary. You can use scissors to cut out shapes, and you can get some interesting effects by contrasting sharp cut edges with softer torn edges.

I paste the paper shapes on to the base using PVA white glue. You can buy this inexpensive water-soluble glue in art and craft shops, or in toy shops. Diluting the glue to a milky consistency will make it easier to use, and will save money.

I apply the glue to the surface of the form to be decorated, place the paper shape on to the glue, and paste it into place. Only small pieces of paper, which form easily to the shape of the object, should be used. Larger pieces tend to lift away from the base because air bubbles form beneath the dry surface decoration.

The step-by-step instructions show the technique being applied to a papier-mâché bowl, but the same method can be used on wood or cardboard forms.

When decorating a bowl I work on the inside first and then continue the decoration over the rim. This makes it possible to achieve a neat edge and a continuity of pattern. The object is left to dry, then turned over and decorated on the outside.

The object to be decorated will become quite wet during the pasting process. Papier-mâché forms made using the layering method have a tendency to warp, so I use the pulp method for open, unsupported shapes such as bowls and plates. Large pieces of wood or card may also warp and should be sealed before the decoration is applied.

My ideas for the surface decoration come from a variety of sources. Themes for my own work have included flowers, tropical fish, and primitive patterns. I look through books and collect magazine cuttings, postcards, and other pictures to give me ideas for designs. I do not necessarily copy these images, but they act as a starting point from which I can develop my own shapes, colour combinations, and patterns.

It might be helpful to plan the design for a bowl or other object on paper before pasting the torn papers in place. I sometimes even draw the pattern on to the papier-mâché form. If this seems daunting, or too time-consuming, then throw caution to the wind and just get pasting!

Making sheets of hand-made recycled paper and papier-mâché bases or forms, and then combining the two, can take quite a long time. However, there is a lot of satisfaction in making a unique and beautiful object *entirely* from waste paper.

Decorating a bowl with torn paper

1 Brush dilute PVA glue on to the surface of the bowl. Paste a small piece of paper firmly to the bowl, pasting over the paper.

2 Continue to apply the base colour or colours. Work over the edge or rim of the bowl.

3 Fold a sheet of hand-made recycled paper several times and tear out the required shape. It may help to draw the shape on to the paper first. How many shapes you can tear out at one time depends on the thickness of the paper; I can usually manage four.

4 Place the shapes on top of the first layer of paper, and paste over them. Continue to apply the shapes until the design is complete. Leave everything to dry.

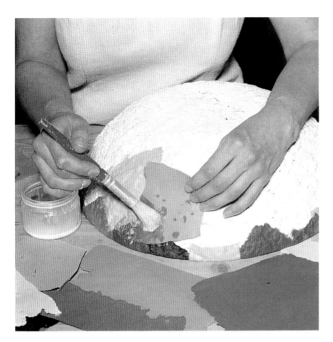

Varnishing

When the bowl is dry it may be sealed or varnished. There is a wide range of varnishes available, giving different finishes from matt to glossy. I use a multi-purpose sealer which you can buy in most DIY stores.

As well as the finish, it is also worth considering whether the varnish will be waterproof enough to let you clean your objects easily. I keep mine clean by dusting them or wiping them with a damp cloth. I would not recommend submerging any papier-mâché form in water.

To stop the paper fading, it is better not to display the object in direct sunlight.

5 When the bowl is dry, turn it over and decorate the underside in the same way as described in stages 1 to 5.

A finished bowl decorated with torn paper and varnished.

Decorating paper, card and wood

The technique of pasting torn paper shapes on to a papier-mâché form can easily be adapted for a flat surface. By collaging hand-made paper on to paper, card and wood you can make a variety of objects, including greetings cards, bookmarks, gift boxes and pictures.

If I have to use wood as a base for a collage I use a good-quality plywood. If you are in any doubt, seal the wood with undercoat paint to prevent it warping. Alternatively, you can attach wooden battens to the back of the collage to hold it rigid.

Cardboard and wood will not cockle, but may warp. To reduce the chance of this happening, you can laminate corrugated cardboard for

Collage on wood.

strength by simply sticking several layers together. I always use double corrugated card from strong boxes if I can.

When collaging on to a sheet of paper it is a good idea to 'stretch' the paper first, or it might cockle as it dries.

To stretch paper, soak a sheet of cartridge paper in water for a few minutes and then place it on a wooden board. Next, carefully ease out any creases and air bubbles from the wet sheet before taping it on to the board with gum strip. (Gum strip is a paper tape with dry gum on one side which becomes sticky when dampened. You can get it in art and craft shops, or stationers').

When the paper dries it will be taut and held flat while the coloured papers are collaged on to it, then when the collage is dry it can be cut from the board.

Collaged greetings card.

Thank-you card.

*A selection of
collaged
greetings cards.*

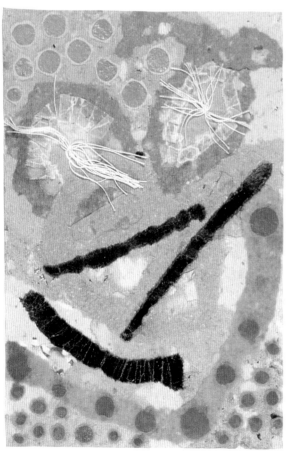

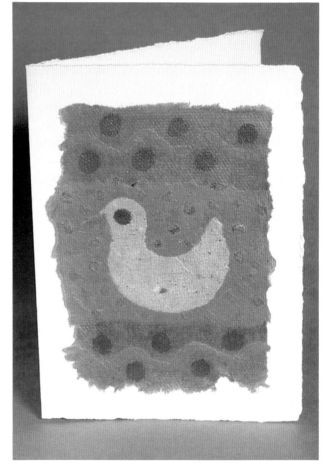

Other materials for collage

For my collages, as well as using plain and decorative hand-made papers I also use other materials, such as metal foils and waxed papers.

Foils

These foils are actually sweet- and chocolate-wrappers which, when cut into small pieces and stuck to the decorative surfaces, provide a shiny contrast to the matt papers. By using lots of small pieces of foil you can make a mosaic-like pattern.

Clocks and a mirror decorated with tiny pieces of coloured foil.

I pick up the small pieces of foil on the end of a damp cocktail stick or matchstick and press them on to undiluted PVA glue on the surface of the object being decorated. Be warned – this process takes ages and is very fiddly!

Waxed papers

Waxed papers offer interesting textures to work with. You can drip hot candlewax on to the paper to make wax spots which you can then tear from the paper and apply as decoration. Each spot will have a ring of fibres protruding from its edge. (When dripping candlewax on to paper, do take care not to set the paper alight.)

Papers with wax patterns on them can be dip-dyed in food colourings or fabric dyes to produce a batik-like effect. The wax will act as a resist to the dye so that wherever the wax occurs the colour of the paper will remain the same; the rest of the paper will change colour. You can buy a batik tool called a tjanting in good art and craft shops.

You can dip whole sheets of paper into hot wax. A batik wax pot is ideal if you have one; alternatively, you could melt some white candles in an old saucepan.

By holding the paper by the corners, dipping half the sheet, allowing it to cool, and then dipping the other half, it should be possible to wax the whole sheet without waxing your fingers too!

Waxed papers become translucent and are very attractive. They can be crunched, cut, and pierced to produce a variety of effects.

Waxed papers and a papier-mâché box decorated with torn-out wax spots.

Warning

Great care must be taken when melting wax in a saucepan as wax can catch fire. Never leave a wax pot or saucepan of wax unattended.

Children must always be supervised when using wax.

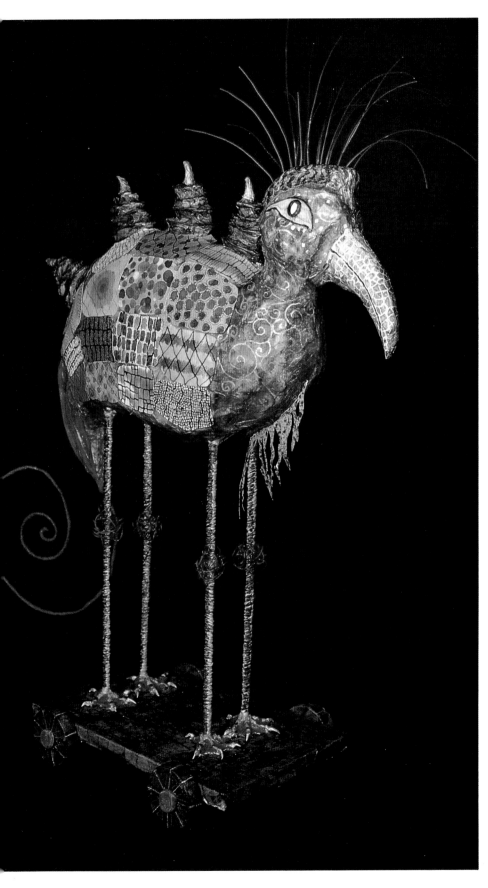

OTHER IDEAS FOR PAPIER MÂCHÉ

Simple forms can be transformed by adding embellishments such as rims, bases and handles. Some basic ideas are illustrated here, but the possibilities are endless. If you experiment with different forms and materials, you will find that you can make quite complicated forms.

A fantasy 'bird' made from papier-mâché.

Chalices

A chalice or goblet form is easy to make – simply join two bowl shapes together. Stick a small bowl on to a larger bowl, with pulp used to conceal the join, so that the two are joined at their bases.

Rims

A rim can be added to a bowl by the following simple method.

First, draw round the top of the bowl on a sheet of cardboard. (I use double corrugated card as it is stronger). Then draw a larger circle to mark the width of rim you want. Cut out the rim just inside the smaller circle to ensure a tight fit. Fill in any gaps between the card rim and the papier-mâché bowl with fine pulp.

Now cover the rim on both sides with a few layers of papier mâché. Allow the forms to dry thoroughly before decorating.

The edges of bowls and rims need not be even, and they can be cut to produce interesting shapes. You can add areas of relief by building them up in pulp, or by layering over string, and you can add handles using cardboard or wire.

Jewellery

Papier mâché is well suited to the making of jewellery. It is an inexpensive material to use, and even large pieces will be light to wear.

You can make simple brooches (opposite page) by cutting shapes from corrugated card and covering them with several layers of papier mâché. When they are dry, you can decorate them using various techniques, and then simply glue a brooch-pin to the back.

You can make large earrings in the same way as the brooches and finish them with the appropriate fixings, while bracelets (below) are easy to make by moulding pulp around the barrels of cling-film-covered glass jars or bottles. Make sure that the jar or bottle does not have a raised ring, or it will be impossible to slide the papier mâché from it once it is dry.

Mirrors and frames

You can make picture frames and decorative mirrors by applying layers of paper and paste to card formers.

To make frames I cut the required shape from corrugated card – double corrugated, if it is available. Several thicknesses may be needed to create the required depth, and I tend to use simple square or rectangular forms, as they work well with my complicated patterns.

Before decorating the frame, you can add interesting embellishments such as fancy tops and raised areas if you like.

Clocks and boxes

The technique used to make a box can easily be adapted to make a simple clock, or a jewellery box. You could add a relief pattern by modelling with pulp, or by layering over string formers. Hinged or loose lids, handles, or little wooden feet would all be interesting additions.

Different-shaped boxes, clocks, and sculptures can all be made by cutting, folding and scoring the card.

To make a clock, cut five pieces of card to make the base and sides of a box, and glue them together, as shown below. Cover the box with several layers of papier mâché to strengthen it.

When it is dry, decorate the box with coloured paper, then drill a hole through the centre of the clockface to take the spindle for the hands. Glue the clock movement, which can be bought from any good craft shop, into place inside the box so that the spindle protrudes through the face. The metal hands which are supplied with the movement can be covered with coloured papers and fixed in place when dry, while you can make feet from short sections of balsa wood covered in coloured paper.

Making the basic box from card.

Papier-mâché sculpture

The versatility of papier mâché makes it an ideal material for sculpture. For larger-scale pieces it provides an inexpensive material with which to express ideas, and it is also light and easy to work with.

A cardboard former can be used in the same way as you would make a clock; by cutting, folding, and scoring card, you can make some quite complex shapes. A large, complex item, though, will need some sort of stable internal framework or armature made from card, wood or chicken-wire. An example of this kind of work is the big bird shown on page 41.

The method I describe here is only an introduction to making sculptural forms: you can of course adapt and develop it to make a form of your own choice.

On the opposite page you can see how easy it is to make a simple fish.

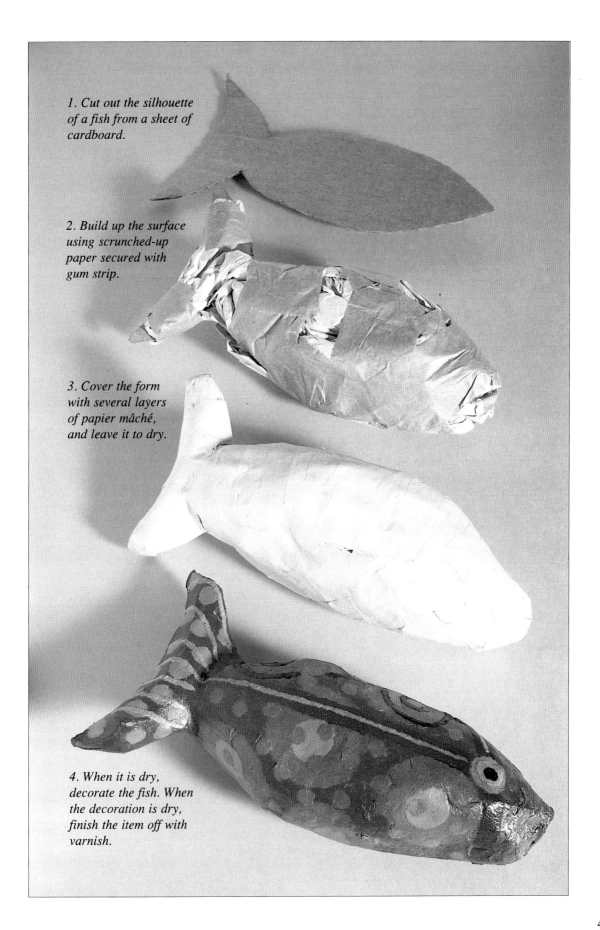

1. Cut out the silhouette of a fish from a sheet of cardboard.

2. Build up the surface using scrunched-up paper secured with gum strip.

3. Cover the form with several layers of papier mâché, and leave it to dry.

4. When it is dry, decorate the fish. When the decoration is dry, finish the item off with varnish.

INDEX